SHE STARTED IT!

A BABY BLUES Cartoon Collection

Rick Kirkman and Jerry Scott
Foreword by Lynn Johnston

CB

CONTEMPORARY
BOOKS

CHICAGO

Library of Congress Cataloging-in-Publication Data

Kirkman, Rick.
    [Baby blues.   Selections]
    She started it! : a Baby blues cartoon
collection / Rick Kirkman and Jerry Scott ;
foreword by Lynn Johnston.
       p.   cm.
    ISBN 0-8092-3896-9 (paper)
    I. Scott, Jerry, 1955– .   II. Title.
III. Title: Baby blues.
PN6728.B25K57   1992
741.5′973—dc20   91-42448
                         CIP

Published by Contemporary Books, Inc.
180 North Michigan Avenue, Chicago, Illinois 60601
Manufactured in the United States of America
International Standard Book Number: 0-8092-3896-9

To Sukey, always.
                    R.K.

To Mom and Pop with love.
                    J.S.

Foreword

When it was announced two years ago that a new "family" comic strip was about to be launched, a well-acquainted rabble of cartoonists waited with anxious curiosity to see what the blessed union of Jerry Scott and Rick Kirkman would produce. Having known them both for some time (and having seen them in action on a number of memorable partying occasions), we knew they were capable of just about anything . . . which is now evident from the howling success of "Baby Blues."

From their mutual pens' has emerged one of the truest and funniest accounts of raising a baby ever to grace the comics page. It's also a kind and contemporary glimpse into the lives of a nurturing couple who, once bent on "doing everything right," are now merely bent—and doing the best they can.

Naturally, we cartoonists welcomed this new comic strip with open admiration. ("Damn. They're good.") No two families are alike, however, even in the comics. Although we cover some of the same territory and discuss similar subjects, we do so from varied and differing points of view, dredging up scenes from our pasts and often revealing more about ourselves in our work than we sometimes care to. (I worry about these guys.) More friends than rivals, we are part of an ever-widening self-help group whose motto goes beyond "a picture is worth a thousand words." We get to write the words as well. This is therapy, and we're willing to share it all.

Having said this, it is my great pleasure to introduce the second published collection of wonderful whinings and witticisms from the creators of "Baby Blues."

Put the kids to bed,
put your feet up,
and, knowing that you're
not alone . . . read on!

Lynn Johnston
Creator, "For Better or for Worse"

BABY BLUES®

RICK KIRKMAN / BY JERRY SCOTT

6

BABY BLUES®

RICK KIRKMAN / BY JERRY SCOTT

FOUR FACES ZOE RECOGNIZES

MOMMY

BEAR

KITTY

DADDY

YOU KNOW YOU'RE REALLY A PARENT WHEN YOU LOOK MORE NATURAL WITH A DIAPER ON YOUR SHOULDER THAN WITHOUT IT.

BABY BLUES®

RICK KIRKMAN / BY JERRY SCOTT

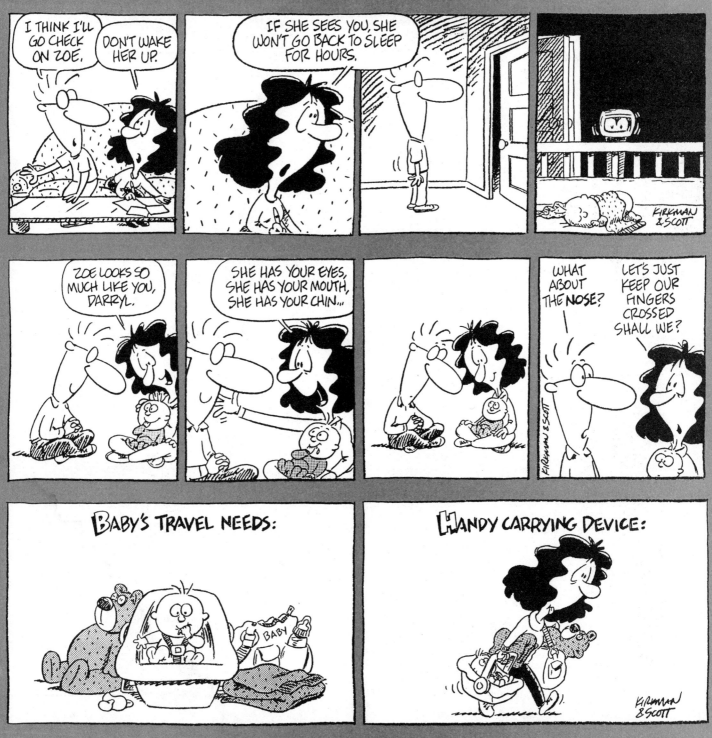

21

22

24

25

28

31

BABY BLUES®

BY RICK KIRKMAN / JERRY SCOTT

2:00 A.M. COME ON, ZOE... ARE YOU GOING TO DO THIS ALL NIGHT?

WAAAA!

YOU KNOW, THEY SAY THAT SOMETIMES YOU JUST HAVE TO LET BABIES CRY THEMSELVES TO SLEEP.

YOU MEAN JUST **LEAVE** HER IN HERE?!

WE'VE TRIED EVERYTHING ELSE!

OOOH... I DON'T KNOW...

COME ON... WE'LL JUST WAIT OUTSIDE THE DOOR FOR A COUPLE OF MINUTES AND SEE WHAT HAPPENS.

WAA! WAA! WAA! WAAAAAAAAA!

WAAAAAA!

THIS ISN'T WORKING.

WAAAAAAAAAAAA!

IN FACT, I THINK IT'S GETTING LOUDER.

KIRKMAN & SCOTT

33

BABY BLUES®

BY RICK KIRKMAN / JERRY SCOTT

36

37

39

40

45

46

48

51

BABY BLUES®

RICK KIRKMAN / BY / JERRY SCOTT

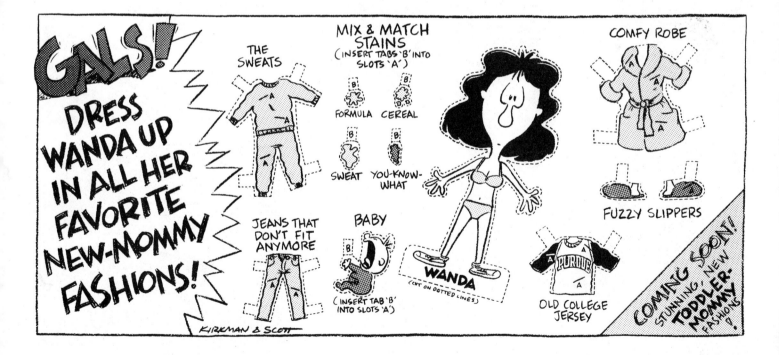

GALS!

DRESS WANDA UP IN ALL HER FAVORITE NEW-MOMMY FASHIONS!

THE SWEATS

MIX & MATCH STAINS
(INSERT TABS 'B' INTO SLOTS 'A')

FORMULA   CEREAL

SWEAT   YOU-KNOW-WHAT

COMFY ROBE

FUZZY SLIPPERS

JEANS THAT DON'T FIT ANYMORE

BABY
(INSERT TAB 'B' INTO SLOTS 'A')

WANDA
(CUT ON DOTTED LINES)

PURDUE

OLD COLLEGE JERSEY

COMING SOON! STUNNING, NEW TODDLER-MOMMY FASHIONS!

KIRKMAN & SCOTT

53

57

60

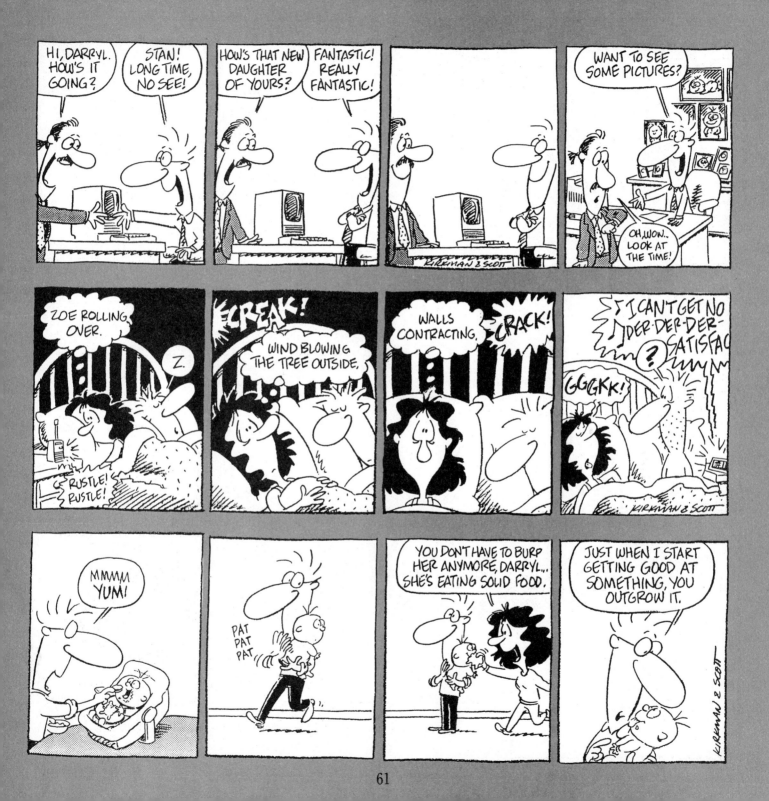

61

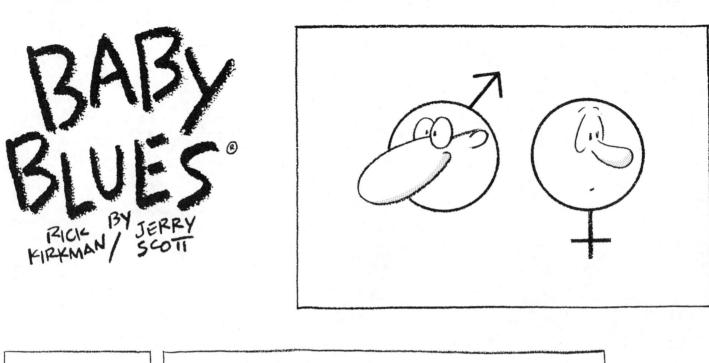

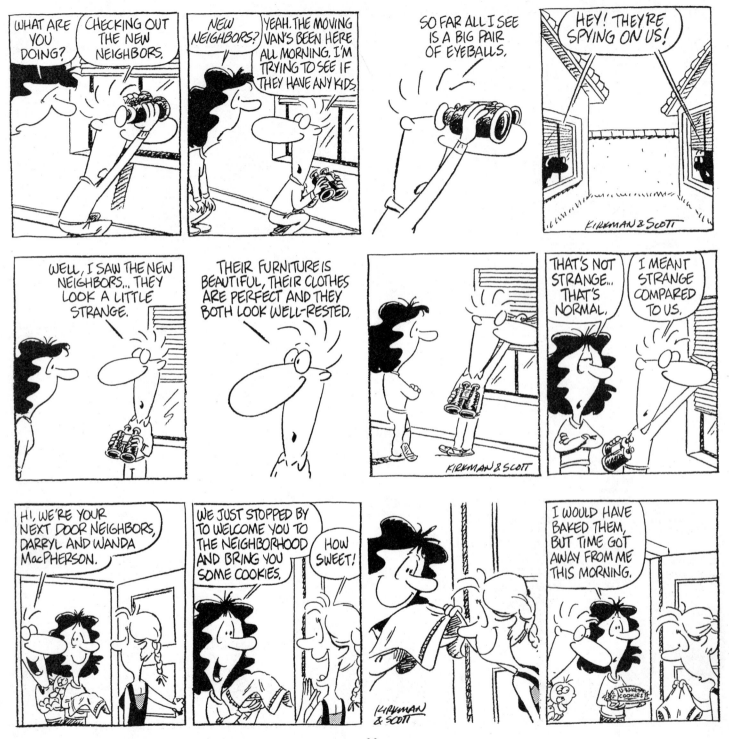

BABY BLUES

RICK KIRKMAN / JERRY SCOTT

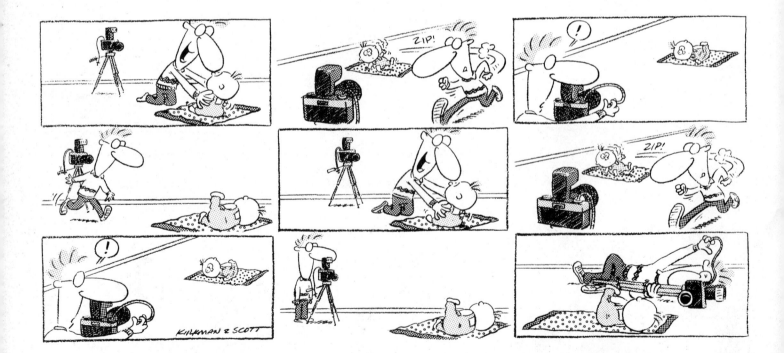

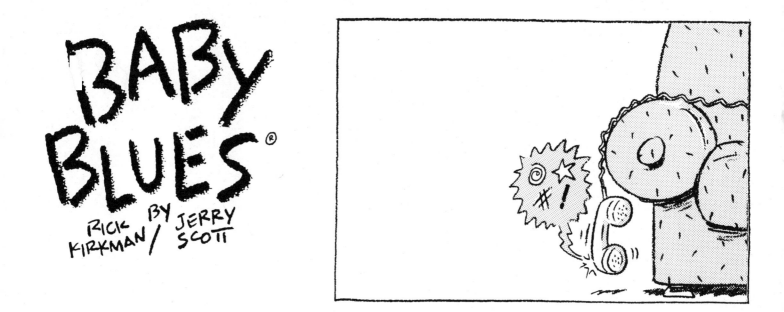

BABY BLUES®

BY RICK KIRKMAN / JERRY SCOTT

UH, SORRY WE'RE LATE.

YOU KNOW HOW WE ALWAYS SEEM TO BE LATE WHEREVER WE GO?

YEAH.

I THINK IT'S BECAUSE WE DON'T PLAN AHEAD.

I'VE MADE A LIST OF ALL THE THINGS WE NEED TO DO SO WE CAN GO OUT TONIGHT, AND I ASSIGNED AN ESTIMATED AMOUNT OF TIME TO COMPLETE EACH TASK.

NOW ALL WE HAVE TO DO IS ADD UP THE TASK TIMES, SUBTRACT THAT TOTAL FROM THE TIME WE'RE SUPPOSED TO LEAVE, AND THAT'S WHAT TIME WE SHOULD START GETTING READY!

SMART IDEA.

SO WHAT TIME SHOULD WE START GETTING READY?

SOMETIME LAST TUESDAY.

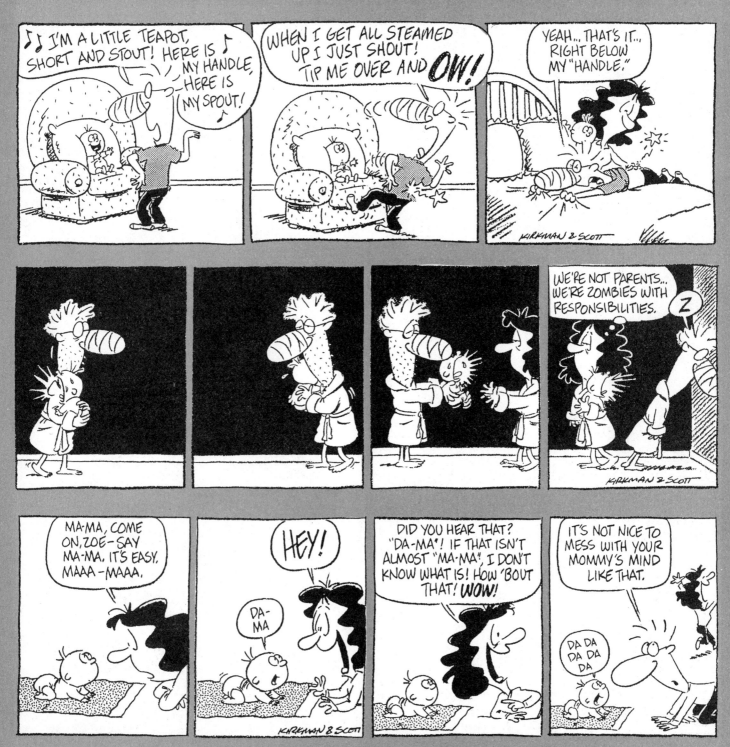

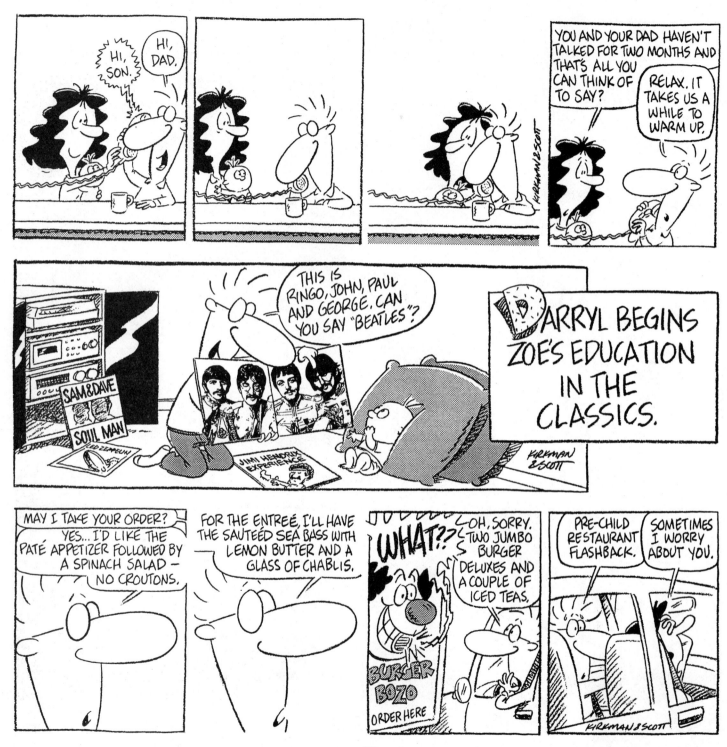

87

88

91

94

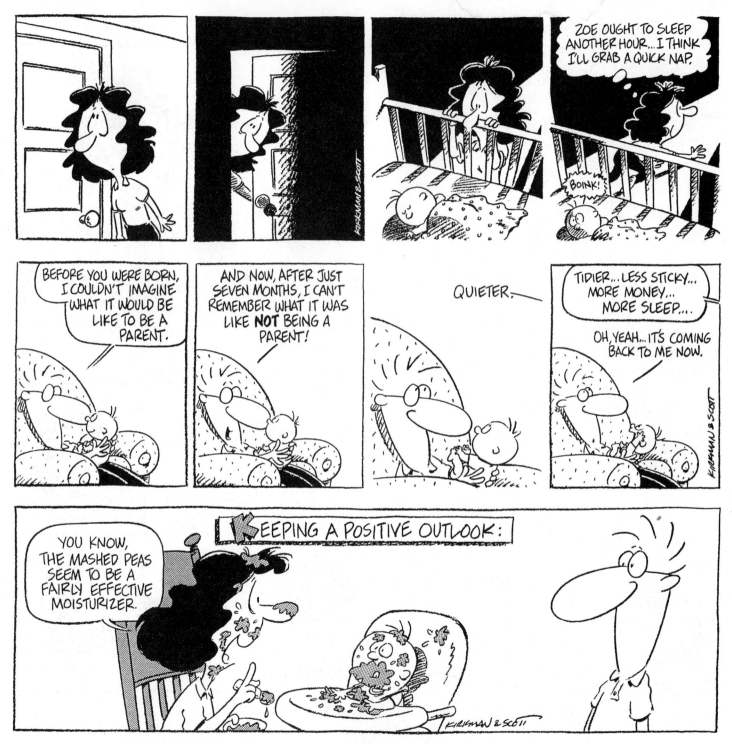

102

108

117

118

BABY BLUES®

BY RICK KIRKMAN / JERRY SCOTT

SHIFTING DESIRES

NO! STAY ON THE BLANKET!

NOT SO FAST! BE CAREFUL!

NO! NO! NOT THAT WAY!

EASY! EASY!

YOU KNOW, I DON'T THINK ZOE IS CRAWLING AS MUCH AS SHE'S SUPPOSED TO.

I LOVE BEING A MOTHER.

I'M PROUD OF BEING A MOTHER.

I'LL ALWAYS BE A MOTHER.

I JUST DON'T WANT TO **LOOK** LIKE ONE!

KIRKMAN & SCOTT

123

Celebrate the birth of a family.

These books are available in your local bookstore or by mail. To order directly, return the coupon below with payment to: Contemporary Books, Customer Service Department, 180 North Michigan Avenue, Chicago, Illinois 60601. Or call (312) 782-9181 to order with your credit card.

Qty.	Title/Author	Price	Total
____	*Baby Blues®: This is going to be tougher than we thought.* by Rick Kirkman and Jerry Scott (3996-5)	$7.95 ea.	$_____
____	*She Started It! A Baby Blues® Cartoon Collection* by Rick Kirkman and Jerry Scott (3896-9)	$7.95 ea.	$_____
		Subtotal	$_____

Add $2.50 postage for the first book ordered. $ _2.50_

Add $1.50 postage for each additional book ordered. $_____

Illinois residents add 7% sales tax; California residents add 6% sales tax. $_____

☐ Enclosed is my check/money order payable to Contemporary Books.   **Total Price** $_____

Bill my ☐ VISA   Account No. _____   Expiration Date _____

☐ MasterCard   Signature _____

Name _____

Address _____

City/State/Zip _____

For quantity discount information, please call the sales department at (312) 782-9181. Allow four to six weeks for delivery. *Offer expires March 31, 1993.*   SST0392